RULES *for* MY SON

*Let's get some things straight
before I get old and uncool.*

RULES *for* MY SON

Indispensable advice from
someone who's been there

WALKER LAMOND

Atlantic Books
London

First published as *Rules for My Unborn Son* in the United States in 2009 by St Martin's Press, an imprint of Macmillan Publishers.

First published in Great Britain in 2016 by Atlantic Books, an imprint of Atlantic Books Ltd.

10 9 8 7 6 5 4 3 2 1

A CIP catalogue record for this book is available from the British Library.

Hardback ISBN: 978 1 78649 0 087
E-book ISBN: 978 1 78649 0 094

Printed in Italy by 🐌 Grafica Veneta S.p.A.

Atlantic Books
An Imprint of Atlantic Books Ltd
Ormond House
26–27 Boswell Street
London
WC1N 3JZ

www.atlantic-books.co.uk

for ARTHUR

INTRODUCTION

*B*oys need rules. *No Spitting. No Swimming. No Fighting.* We don't always like them, but for the most part, they are necessary. Rules keep us safe, eliminate uncertainty, and encourage harmonious social interaction. *Yield to Pedestrians. Black Tie Required.* They are the simplest and most effective way to pass down tried and true institutional knowledge through the generations. In short, rules are GOOD!

But somewhere along the way, rules got a bad name. People wanted freedom. Authority was questioned, rules were broken, dress codes banished! Rules were seen as antiquated obstacles to individualism and progress. Barbers were ignored, ties packed away. And the game of life suddenly got a bit sloppier, more uncertain, and even a bit less fun.

My father rarely wore socks, a sartorial quirk made permissible by the fact he was often the best-dressed gentleman in the room. This perhaps best exemplifies his approach to life. A vigorous dancer, a dedicated sportsman, and the tireless life of any party, he understood that a man of strong character, who took pride in his appearance and behaviour, was given the most liberty to have fun. And so he had rules. Many of them came from his father, and presumably his father before that. They governed everything from his dress to his business dealings and were based on the notion that there are certain things a Good Man does and certain things he does not do. My father was a Good Man. And he was the kind of father I aspired to be. He passed away shortly after my twenty-second birthday.

This small book began simply as a way to preserve the lessons my father had taught me and perhaps, add my spin on what makes a Good Man. I hoped to have a son of my own one day, so I thought it best to write it all down before the mayhem of actual fatherhood made me too soft or too sanctimonious, and most importantly, before my own childhood was too distant in the rear-view mirror. It would be a father-to-be's promise to his unborn son: 'To get some things straight before I get old and uncool'.

Of course, the list needed a bit of updating. My dad could fold a mean pocket square, but he didn't have much to offer on Internet etiquette. As the list grew, however, what struck me was how many of my father's rules stood up unchanged – even for a recovering hipster living in New York. *Rules for My Son* became a set of instructions for being a good man and a good father, not just a list of commandments for any future progeny.

My father and I are not the first men to attempt to define and defend the qualities that make up the modern gentleman. In the book I acknowledge the influences of some very fine men who have offered wise and practical advice through the ages either through their words (George Orwell, Buckminster Fuller, Mark Twain) or their example (Fred Astaire, Mick Jagger, David Bowie). Some of the advice the reader may have heard before. And I should hope so, as many of the rules are distillations of some universal lessons in ethics and etiquette. I have made efforts to cull the classics from the outmoded. After all, not all that is old is good. However, what I hope makes *Rules for My Son* unique is the inclusion of lessons drawn from my own experiences – the good, the bad, and the ugly. The rules included herein may evoke from the reader a hearty endorsement or a spirited objection. Or perhaps inspire a sentimental journey back into the reader's own childhood. And maybe, for a particular kind of discerning young parent, *Rules for My Son* will be just what it says it is – a good old-fashioned book of rules for you and your family. I hope it proves useful.

Walker Lamond
Washington, D.C.

When in doubt, wear a tie.

Ride in the front car
of a roller coaster.

See movies on the big screen.

—◦◦◦—

Men with facial hair have something to hide.

—◦◦◦—

Be a vigorous dancer.

*However, you're under no obligation
to join a conga line.*

Be a strong swimmer,
especially in the ocean.

—⁘—

Avoid gossip.

—⁘—

Don't waste time with
a fancy watch.

—◦◦◦—

Talent is learned.
Learn to sing.

—◦◦◦—

Stand up for the little guy.
He'll remember you.

—◦◦◦—

We are what we pretend to be,
so we must be careful about
what we pretend to be.

KURT VONNEGUT

Avoid affectations,
lest they become
habits.

Buy seasonal fruit from
your local market or
greengrocer.

Don't attempt a dialect other than your own,

unless it's in the script.

Men should not wear sandals.

Ever.

On stage is no time to be shy.

❦

Speak up.

Start a band.

———ᵒⁿᵒ———

A T-shirt is neither
a philosophy nor an
advertisement. It's a shirt.
Wear it plain.

———ᵒⁿᵒ———

Know her dress size.
Don't ask.

—⟋⟍⟋⟍⟋—

On occasion, pick up the tab.

—⟋⟍⟋⟍⟋—

Don't poke fun at
contemporary art.
Put it in context.

—⟋⟍⟋⟍⟋—

Don't spit on the

pavement.

⁓

The key to good
photography is not
timing. It's editing.

⁓

Don't be shy in the changing room.
They are all thinking the same thing.

Be a good listener.
Don't just wait your turn to talk.

A vandal is the lowest
form of scoundrel.

——∞∞——

Yes Ma'am. No Sir.
No exceptions.

——∞∞——

Spend time with your mother.

❦

She's cooler than you think.

Choose your corner, pick away at it carefully, intensely, and to the best of your ability, and that way you might change the world.

CHARLES EAMES

Know your furniture.
But never buy it all at once.

On a road trip, offer to buy
the first tank of petrol.

Shorts are for little boys. Decide
for yourself when you are a man.

Always meet your date at the door.

—∞∞—

Make a rock and roll pilgrimage.

—∞∞—

Make a hipster's day.
Donate old clothes
to charity.

Close the door,
turn it up,
dork out.

Audition for a play.
Read for the lead.

—◦◦◦—

Never pack more than
you can carry yourself.

—◦◦◦—

Live in the city,
briefly.

—◦◦◦—

Offer to carry a woman's bags.

Especially your mother's.

Take the stairs.

Root for the home team,
even when they stink.

Have a reliable hangout.

Nothing good ever happens after 3 A.M.
I promise.

Sit in the front of the classroom.

Finish what you start,
especially books.

There is rarely a time to raise your voice.
At the football is one.

Never eat the same
meal twice in a row.

Don't show off.
Impress.

Make sure your clothes fit properly.

A human being should be able to change a diaper, plan an invasion, butcher a hog, conn a ship, design a building, write a sonnet, balance accounts, build a wall, set a bone, comfort the dying, take orders, give orders, cooperate, act alone, solve equations, analyze a new problem, pitch manure, program a computer, cook a tasty meal, fight efficiently, die gallantly. Specialization is for insects.

ROBERT ANSON HEINLEIN

Don't message a selfie you wouldn't
be happy to show your mother.

Don't loiter where there
is a dispute that does not
concern you.

Don't be a mooch.

When speaking with a journalist, choose your words carefully.

Think about your answers,
then call them back.

Push-ups and sit-ups
are all you'll ever need to
build muscle.

⟶ ∽ ⟵

Never criticize a
book, play, or film
unless you have read
or seen it yourself.
Art is full of surprises.

⟶ ∽ ⟵

Support friends in the arts.
Especially if they stink.

———◦◦◦———

Learn to sail.

———◦◦◦———

The most expensive
restaurant is never
the best.

———◦◦◦———

Remember, the girl you're with
is somebody's sister. And he's
perfectly capable of beating you up.

Be a good passer, but
don't forget to shoot.

Every time I see an adult on a bicycle, I no longer despair for the future of the human race.

H. G. WELLS

Wear a blazer when travelling by plane. It has easily accessible pockets.

————∾∾————

Spend as much time as you can on the water. In a pinch, even a creek will do.

————∾∾————

Keep your word.

Never side against
your brother in a fight.

Memorize your favourite poem.

Respect fire.

Philanthropy is not measured in notes and coins.

Never go out of your way to be on TV.

—◦◦◦—

On a city pavement, walk briskly and don't impede pedestrian traffic.

—◦◦◦—

Never hog a microphone.

—◦◦◦—

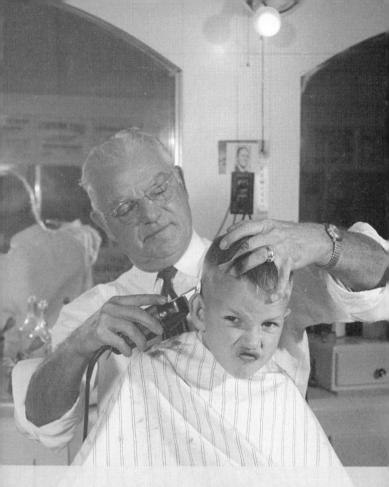

Don't spend too much money
on a haircut.

❧⦿❧

They don't last.

Take the train.

Persevere with olives.
You'll grow to like them.

Let the axe do the work.

—ↄᴑᴑᴐ—

Feel free to crash a
party at a music festival.

—ↄᴑᴑᴐ—

You don't get to choose
your own nickname.

Enough already.
Learn the rules of cricket.

———✎———

If you're going to reinvent yourself,

be original.

———✎———

Bodysurf.

Be subtle.
She sees you.

Give credit.
Take the blame.

Don't underestimate
your fertility.

———∞———

Write down your dreams.

———∞———

When things go wrong — don't go with them.

ELVIS PRESLEY

Keep your guard up.

Unless you have served
in the armed forces,
no camouflage gear.

———◦◦◦———

The best thing you can give your
neighbours is a well-kept lawn.

———◦◦◦———

Keep a schedule.

———◦◦◦———

Experience the serenity
of travelling alone.

The one true measure of
a successful adventure is
returning home safely.

—∞∞∞—

Call your mum.

—∞∞∞—

Your best chance of being a rock
star is learning the bass.

—∞∞∞—

When excusing yourself from the
table, you need not give a reason.

If you have the right of way, take it.

If the maître d' mistakes you
for someone famous, there's
no rush to correct him.

Sympathy is a crutch.
Never fake a limp.

———∞∞∞———

Take your own pictures
at family events.

———∞∞∞———

Don't let the pictures
become the event.

When it comes to
opening presents, no one
likes a good guesser.

⁓

Don't gloat. A good friend will do it for you.

⁓

The good life is one inspired by love and guided by knowledge.

BERTRAND RUSSELL

Don't tip the owner.
A handshake will do.

Don't stare directly
into a dog's eyes.

You can't cram for
a dental exam.

Don't rush.

No coffee until you're sixteen.

Never under any circumstances
ask a woman if she is pregnant.

Make time for your mum on your birthday.

⸺⸺∾∾⸺⸺

It's her special day, too.

Courage is not the lack of fear,

it is acting in spite of it.

MARK TWAIN

Don't date the bartender.

⟋⟋⟍

Learn to pronounce French
words correctly.

⟋⟋⟍

Invest in great luggage.
The world will know that
you've arrived.

⟋⟋⟍

Be a regular at your
local flea market.

Let napping dads lie.

Don't be so eager to leave
the kid's table.

If you choose to wear a tie, commit.
Button your top button.

———✧✧✧———

Offer your date the seat
with the best view of the
restaurant.

———✧✧✧———

Never be the last one in the pool.

Keep a garden.

Surprise your dad at the office.

Trust me, whatever I'm doing is not as important as you.

The essence of being human is that one does not seek perfection.

GEORGE ORWELL

Get back in touch with old friends.

Never turn down an invitation
to speak in public.

Eat more fish.

Do your own bicycle repairs.

——⁓⁓⁓——

Order dessert.

——⁓⁓⁓——

Don't shout out requests at rock concerts.

——⁓⁓⁓——

Have a signature look.

⁓⦿⁓

Be a good wingman.

When selling tickets,
take face value.

Don't stare. People-watch.

Protect your privacy,
especially when you're famous.

Keep your eye on the ball and follow through.

In sports and in life.

When you're grown-up and visit your parents, bring a bottle.

Explore the branches of your family tree. You never know what you might find.

Sleep with the window open.

———∽∽∽———

If you drop change, pick it up.
Even the pennies.

———∽∽∽———

Don't pose with booze.

———∽∽∽———

Make your own costume.

Only those who risk going too far can possibly find out how far one can go.

T.S. Eliot

You aren't done raking until you've played in the leaf pile.

———*ono*———

Never respond to a critic in writing.

———*ono*———

Know the difference between arts and crafts.

———*ono*———

Fish don't have eyelids. Cast into the shade.

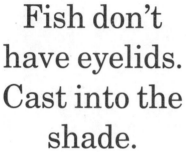

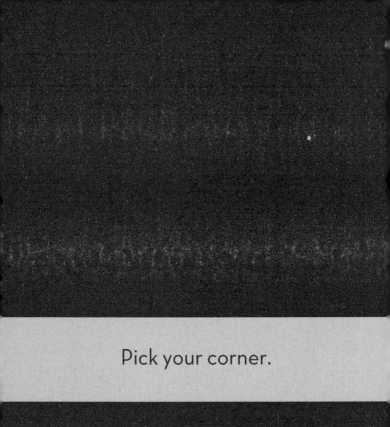

Pick your corner.

Don't settle for a ready-made cake.
Bake!

Surround yourself with smart
people.

Don't be a snob.

It takes a great deal of bravery to stand up to our enemies, but just as much to stand up to our friends.

J.K. ROWLING

When fishing, practice catch

and release.

If the teacher forgets to assign homework,

keep quiet.

Take her picture.

Don't ride your bike on the pavement.

—◦◦◦—

Stand up to bullies.
You'll only have to do it once.

—◦◦◦—

If you've made your point,
stop talking.

———~~~———

Watch your language at the match.

———~~~———

Sit for a portrait.

———~~~———

Always keep a recent photograph of yourself on file in case of emergencies or unexpected notoriety.

Get your pumpkins from
a pumpkin patch.

 Own at least one
bespoke suit.

Have a pen pal.

Admit when you are wrong.
Mean it.

If you spot a teacher outside of school,
leave him or her be.

Don't sabotage the family portrait.

———∞∞∞———

Smile please.

A sensible man ought to find sufficient company in himself.

EMILY BRONTË

Don't personalize your number plates.

—⟶⟳⟵—

If you offer to help, don't quit until the job is done.

—⟶⟳⟵—

When it's time to sing in church, SING!
It's a great time to practice.

Wear freshly cleaned pajamas.

If it looks like rain, carry an umbrella.
She'll thank you.

Cary Grant has no need for Gore-Tex.

The young man knows the rules,
but the old man knows the exceptions.

OLIVER WENDELL HOLMES, SR.

Be precise.

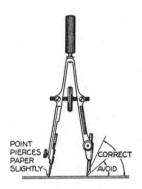

POINT
PIERCES
PAPER
SLIGHTLY

CORRECT

AVOID

Identify your most
commonly used word or phrase
and eliminate it.

Stay busy. There is always
something that could use
a fresh coat of paint.

If you attend a late-night after-party,
have an exit strategy.

On Sunday morning,
a gentleman gets dressed.

Remember, it's the first day of the week, not the last.

There is never an excuse
for stealing someone's taxi.

When you're older,
teach.

Look people in the eye when you
thank them, especially waiters.

—∞∞—

Choose a window seat
and enjoy the view.

—∞∞—

Twice a year, write
down your goals.

—∞∞—

No gang is complete
without one cool girl.

———∞∞∞———

Hang artwork
at eye level.

———∞∞∞———

There is no need to tell anyone
you are leaving the bar.

———∞∞∞———

Always do sober what you said you'd do drunk. That will teach you to keep your mouth shut.

ERNEST HEMINGWAY

Keep a well-stocked bar.

———◦◦◦———

Read before bed every night.

———◦◦◦———

Pick a font and stick to it.

———◦◦◦———

You will have a love life one day.

Be discreet.

Don't throw sand or, when
you're older, mud.

———∽∽∽———

Don't panic.

———∽∽∽———

When singing karaoke,
choose a song in your range.

———∽∽∽———

Thank the bus driver.

———⚬⚬⚬———

Go down fighting.

———⚬⚬⚬———

If you're playing a poker game and you look around the table and can't tell who the sucker is, it's you.

PAUL NEWMAN

Keep your passport current.

———◦⁄◦◦⁄◦———

Become an expert in something.

———◦⁄◦◦⁄◦———

Write letters.
On paper.

———◦⁄◦◦⁄◦———

Be careful what you put in writing. You can't take it back.

=∞=

There is exactly one place where it is acceptable to wear gym clothes.

=∞=

*Mr. Bowie preferred trousers
to tracksuits.*

Never ask about another person's grades or salary.

To execute a proper rugby tackle, lower your shoulder, not your head.

Cite your sources,
even online.

———◦◦◦———

Whistle.

———◦◦◦———

Never push someone off a dock.
The view is better when you're not
afraid of who is behind you.

———◦◦◦———

Offer to take a stranger's picture.

Work quickly.

Help a buddy move.

—∽∾∽—

Don't boast about projects in progress.
Celebrate their completion.

—∽∾∽—

Until you are a doctor, never
answer your phone at the table.

—∞∞—

If you make a mistake,
forgive yourself and move on.

—∞∞—

Be a good diver.

—∞∞—

Grace is an underappreciated
quality in men.

When you are a houseguest, be
sure to wake up before your hosts.

After lighting a firecracker,
stand back.

In a canoe, do your share of the work.

Go barefoot. It toughens the feet.

Make yourself useful on a boat.
If you can't tie knots, fetch the beers.

Spend a summer waiting tables.

—⁓—

Always keep a good joke handy.

—⁓—

Take your sunglasses off indoors. This includes elevators and planes.

—⁓—

Don't salt your food until
you've tasted it.

Never turn
down a girl's
invitation to
dance.

Be true to your school.

BRIAN WILSON

Pull a sickie
once a year.

Never skip practice.

Avoid air-conditioning.

Order the local speciality.

―――ᔆᔆᔆ―――

Don't boo.
Even the ref is somebody's son.

―――ᔆᔆᔆ―――

Enter a talent show.

Be like a duck.
Remain calm on the surface
and paddle like hell underneath.

MICHAEL CAINE

Drive across the country.
Don't rush.

Limit your time in the sauna.

Never ask to be taken
out of a ball game.

You don't need your
phone to sleep. It will still
be there tomorrow.

———◦◦◦———

There's nothing wrong with musical
theatre. Everything in moderation.

———◦◦◦———

Chicks dig Gershwin.

Don't have a girlfriend
at university.

—◦◦◦—

A man's luggage doesn't roll.

—◦◦◦—

Don't drive an automatic.

—◦◦◦—

Jump in with your clothes on.

———∞———

Smile at pretty girls.

———∞———

A wise man knows his way
around a kitchen.

Have a signature dish,
even if it's your only one.

———∞∞∞———

Be quick with a 'Good morning'.

———∞∞∞———

Have a favourite song.
It doesn't have to be cool.

———∞∞∞———

Be careful not to ogle
girls at the beach. That's
what sunglasses are for.

—∞∞—

If you ignore
history, it will
ignore you.

—∞∞—

If you get yourself arrested, call me.

~~

You get one free pass.

Drive a fuel-efficient car.

~~~

Don't be afraid to nominate yourself.
Be up to the task.

~~~

Make curfew.
Sneak out later to meet her.

~~~

A museum is a great place
to beat a hangover.
It's cool, quiet, and full of
water fountains.

—⌘—

Keep your room
clean.
One day you'll have a
girlfriend.

—⌘—

Do your washing often.
You won't need as
many clothes.

———∞∞∞———

Never leave a job without
securing your next
employment.

———∞∞∞———

But when it's time to go,
don't hesitate.

———∞∞∞———

To have a right to do a thing is not at all the same as to be right in doing it.

G.K. CHESTERTON

When it comes to shovelling snow, the earlier you start, the easier the job.

Be nice to your sister.
You are her cheerleader, confidante,
and bodyguard.

———⦿———

Find yourself a
good hideout.

———⦿———

Don't be afraid to cry
at a good movie.

———⦿———

Don't get a dog if you don't have time to walk it.

Know the proper
time to wear a tuxedo.
It's more often than you think.

The keys to throwing a
good party are a working
stereo, Christmas lights,
and plenty of ice.

Be cool to the younger kids.
Reputations are built over a lifetime.

―⟨≈⟩―

Drive a classic car before you are thirty.
Be able to fix it yourself.

―⟨≈⟩―

Be confident on the underground.

―⟨≈⟩―

On a night out with the boys,
never be the first to go home.

———⟨∞⟩———

If you're going to quote someone,
get it right.

———⟨∞⟩———

Know the proper time to chew
gum. It's less often than you think.

—∞∞∞—

On occasion, go to the
movies by yourself.

—∞∞∞—

Wait for your song to play
on the jukebox.

—∞∞∞—

Here's a rule I recommend.
Never practice two vices at once.

TALLULAH BANKHEAD

Find your favourite painting.

—∞∞∞—

Travelling to a foreign city is an
excuse to dress up, not down.

—∞∞∞—

Dance with your partner, not at her.

But don't forget to lead.

The best thing to do in the rain
is be quiet and listen.

—⁓—

Go all out on
Halloween.

—⁓—

Ask your mother
to dance.

—⁓—

Take the time to
polish your shoes.

———ഹ———

Don't get fancy
about your
beer or coffee.

———ഹ———

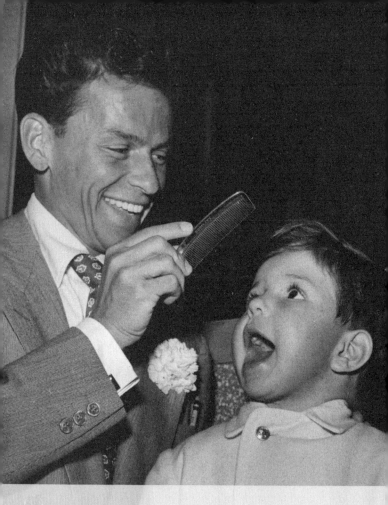

Try a hairstyle you'll one day regret.

I'll get over it.

Don't let the ice-cream van get away.

—∞—

Despite what your may hear, not everyone's a winner. It doesn't mean you shouldn't play.

—∞—

Don't lose your cool.
Especially at work.

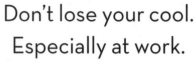

Skip the second cheapest wine on the menu.
It's usually bad.

Participate in a
good practical joke.

When handling a frog, be gentle.

Offer your name when greeting someone. Even good friends have lousy memories.

———◦◦◦———

Be able to identify all of the trees on your block.

———◦◦◦———

It is no use saying,
'We are doing our best'.
You have got to succeed in doing
what is necessary.

WINSTON CHURCHILL

Don't skip breakfast.

Hustle.

If your mother is watching,
wear a helmet.

Keep hardback copies of your
favourite books. Donate the rest to a
local exchange.

⟨⟨⟨⟩⟩⟩

Treat your body well.
You'll be glad you did
when you are a dad.

⟨⟨⟨⟩⟩⟩

Be beholden to no one.
Pay in cash.

Remember to thank your hosts.

If you don't know what
a word means, ask.
Before it's too late.

———⁓⁓⁓———

Know your
neighbourhood like
the back of your hand.
Sometimes the best
adventures are in your
own backyard.

———⁓⁓⁓———

There is no better
remedy than a dip in the
ocean.

━━━∞∞∞━━━

Trust the
concierge.

━━━∞∞∞━━━

Marry the girl, you marry
the whole family.

⟨⟨⟨⟩⟩⟩

Never request a joke or impression.
They are never as good on
command.

Suck it up.

If you have to make more
than one substitution,
order something else.

———oⁱo———

Wisdom begins with
an awe of nature.

———oⁱo———

Wit ought to be a glorious treat like caviar; never spread it about like marmalade.

NOËL COWARD

Attend lots of weddings.
Your friends will be there
and the food is always
good.

—⚬⚬⚬—

Send postcards.

—⚬⚬⚬—

Read the good majority of a
newspaper every day.

⟋⟍⟋⟍⟋⟍

Don't forget the
funny pages.

⟋⟍⟋⟍⟋⟍

Collect things.

Draw what you see, not what you think is there.

Exercise in the morning. Cycling to school or work is a good idea.

Socks are not necessary in the
summer,
no matter how formal the occasion.

Use a griddle.
It's an indoor BBQ.

Befriend your local
butcher.

—∞—

Sign the
guestbook.

—∞—

Own your own
golf clubs. All other
athletic equipment can
be shared or borrowed.

Offer your seat
to a woman, no matter
how old she is.

Get to know your
sister's boyfriends.

Never criticize the government of your
own country when you are abroad.

Be patient with airline personnel.

It will pay off with better service.

Play park football.

———∞∞∞———

You won't always be the strongest or fastest. You can be the toughest.

———∞∞∞———

An hour with your
grandparents is time
well spent.

—◦◦◦—

In the long run,
loyalty trumps ambition
every time.

—◦◦◦—

Watch a lightning storm from a safe spot. But watch 'em.

—⁓⁓⁓—

When caught in a riptide,
swim parallel to the beach.

—⁓⁓⁓—

Compliment your mum's cooking.

Wrap your own presents.
Kitchen foil works in a pinch and you
don't need tape.

———

Be a well-informed

voter.

———

Don't forget your local elections.

———

It's not worth doing something unless someone, somewhere, would much rather you weren't doing it.

TERRY PRATCHETT

Don't litter.
Ever.

Honking your
horn won't make them
go faster.

Sometimes,
the answer
can't be found
on Google.

———∞∞∞———

Minimize talking on
the telephone.

———∞∞∞———

Don't be afraid of
games you don't know.
It's the best way to
learn.

———◦∞◦———

Keep iced tea in the fridge.
It's healthy, cold, and cheap.

———◦∞◦———

If you can afford it,
own your own tuxedo.

If you absolutely have to fight,
punch first and punch hard.

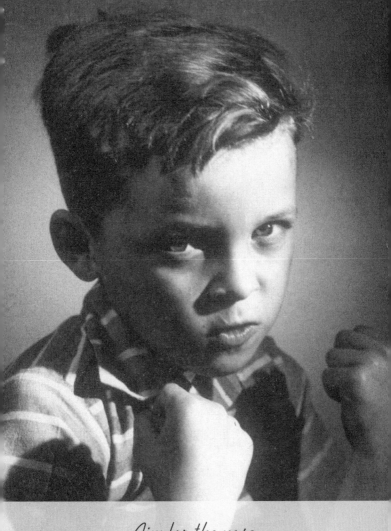

Aim for the nose.

No one likes a know-it-all.

———✦✦✦———

Choose the correct
screwdriver for the job.

———✦✦✦———

When in the woods, be quiet.

Keep a copy of your letters. It will
make it easier on your biographer.

*Never let your correspondence
fall behind.*

ABRAHAM LINCOLN

Eat more vegetables.
Takes care of the ticker.

Never talk during a
movie. Arrive early and go
for centre seats.

Respect dress codes.
You'll have more liberty to be funny.

———∞∞∞———

Learn to tie
a bow tie.

———∞∞∞———

Girls like boys who shower.

———∞∞∞———

Write thank-you notes promptly on personalized correspondence cards.

In Monopoly, buy the orange properties.

Don't renege on bets.
Better yet, don't
gamble.

——ᎧᏋᎧ——

When shaking hands,
grip firmly and look him in the eye.

——ᎧᏋᎧ——

Absolutely no piercings or tattoos,
unless you are in the armed forces.

Spend time with your cousins.
You're more alike than you think.

Don't leave the crust.

Just because you're offended,
doesn't mean you're right.

RICKY GERVAIS

You are what you do,
not what you say.

Don't flatten burgers on the BBQ.
It squeezes out all the juices.

It is not enough to
be proud of your
ancestry. Live up to it.

———⟊⟊⟊———

Don't make a
scene.

———⟊⟊⟊———

Learn an instrument, preferably one that can be played at home in the company of friends.

Never switch a seating card.

When building a campfire,
choose deadwood from a tree,
not off the ground.

Keep a scrapbook. But avoid collage.

———&—

Jazz is for dancing.

———&—

Hold doors, pull out chairs,
easy on the swears.

WILL SMITH

Bring a tennis ball to the park.

Finish the crossword.

Don't use a chisel for
anything other than its
intended purpose.

When making an acceptance
speech, keep it short, lose the notes,
and thank your dad.

Don't fight forces, use them.

BUCKMINSTER FULLER

Don't be afraid of a little sun.

Follow instructions.
You'll be done in half the time.

Know when to
ignore the camera.

For of those to whom much is given,
much is required.

LUKE 12:48

Don't be afraid to ask out the
best-looking girl in the room.

———∞∞∞———

When climbing,
use a rope.

———∞∞∞———

Nothing is
more important
than family.

You can never overdress.

APPENDIX

REQUIRED LISTENING
FOR BOYS

- ☐ Pulp . . . . 'Common People'
- ☐ Nat King Cole . . . . 'Straighten Up and Fly Right'
- ☐ A Tribe Called Quest . . . . 'Electric Relaxation'
- ☐ Little Richard. . . . .'Long Tall Sally'
- ☐ The Beatles . . . . 'Twist and Shout'
- ☐ Bob Dylan. . . . .'It's All Over Now, Baby Blue'
- ☐ Four Tops . . . .'Reach Out (I'll Be There)'
- ☐ The Who. . . . .'A Quick One'
- ☐ We Five. . . . . 'You Were On My Mind'
- ☐ The Monkees. . . . . 'Last Train to Clarksville'
- ☐ Otis Redding . . . . 'These Arms of Mine'
- ☐ The Beach Boys . . . .'Good Vibrations'
- ☐ Elvis Presley. . . . .'Suspicious Minds'
- ☐ Jimmy Cliff. . . . .'Many Rivers to Cross'
- ☐ The Faces. . . . . 'Stay With Me'
- ☐ Frank Sinatra . . . . 'My Way'
- ☐ The Rolling Stones . . . .'Waiting on a Friend'

- ❑ Big Star .... 'Thirteen'
- ❑ Tom Waits .... 'Grapefruit Moon'
- ❑ Joni Mitchell .... 'Free Man in Paris'
- ❑ Lyle Lovett .... 'If I Had a Boat'
- ❑ Jackson Browne .... 'These Days'
- ❑ James Brown .... 'I Got You'
- ❑ David Bowie .... 'Life on Mars'
- ❑ Hall & Oates .... 'Rich Girl'
- ❑ Billy Joel .... 'Movin' Out'
- ❑ Queen .... 'Don't Stop Me Now'
- ❑ Elvis Costello .... 'Peace, Love and Understanding'
- ❑ The Ramones .... 'I Wanna Be Your Boyfriend'
- ❑ R.E.M. .... 'Radio Free Europe'
- ❑ Joe Jackson .... 'Step Out'
- ❑ Big Country .... 'In a Big Country'
- ❑ Prince .... 'Let's Go Crazy'
- ❑ The Clash .... 'London Calling'
- ❑ The Pogues .... 'Fairytale of New York'
- ❑ The Smiths .... 'Girlfriend in a Coma'
- ❑ The Who .... 'Who Are You'

ESSENTIAL READING
FOR BOYS

❐ Charles Darwin .... *The Origin of Species*

❐ J.R.R. Tolkien .... *The Hobbit*

❐ F. Scott Fitzgerald .... *The Great Gatsby*

❐ Ernest Hemingway .... *The Old Man and the Sea*

❐ Jostein Gaarder .... *Sophie's World*

❐ George Orwell *1984*

❐ Ken Kesey .... *One Flew Over the Cuckoo's Nest*

❐ Rudyard Kipling .... *Just So Stories*

❐ Michelle Magorian .... *Goodnight Mister Tom*

❐ Patrick O'Brian .... *Master and Commander*

❐ Robert Louis Stevenson.................... *Treasure Island*

❐ E.M. Forster.......................... *A Passage to India*

❐ Fyodor Dostoevsky .... *The Brothers Karamazov*

❐ Michael Morpurgo .... *War Horse*

❐ Richard Yates .... *Revolutionary Road*

❐ James Cain .... *The Postman Always Rings Twice*

❐ Sebastian Junger .... *The Perfect Storm*

❐ Robert M. Pirsig .... *Zen and the Art of Motorcycle Maintenance*

PHOTO CREDITS

ACKNOWLEDGMENTS

I am grateful for the following people and institutions: Tumblr; Laura Wyss, a splendid photo researcher; my dedicated agent, Karen Gerwin; my talented editor, Alyse Diamond; and the entire staff at St. Martin's Press.

A number of people made significant contributions to the writing of this book, none as important as those by my wife, Colleen Lamond; my sister, Lizzy McMurtrie; and my mother, Betsy Lamond, the best teacher and friend a boy could hope for. Each is a testament to the truth that a father can teach you to be a man, but it is the women in your life that keep you alive and well. I am also grateful to my grandfather John C. Walker, a large number of friends whose character and talents inspire me daily, and the thousands of people who shared their own rules and advice for raising a good man.

I am especially grateful for the advice, example, and friendship of my father, Thomas B. Lamond, in whose memory I have dedicated this book.